David Wharton

Thurman Publishing

Mr Tickle was out in the park. It was a sunny day, and the children were on holiday from school.

'What a good day for tickling,' thought Mr Tickle.

A gardener was sweeping up some

dead leaves. Mr Tickle reached out and tickled him. The gardener fell into the pile of leaves.

'It's a good job you had a soft place to fall,' said Mr Tickle.

At the edge of the park there was a group of trees. Mr Bounce was walking under a low bough.

Suddenly a long arm appeared from behind a tree and tickled Mr Bounce, which made him jump! He bounced up to the

bough and hit his head. Poor Mr Bounce!

But as soon as Mr Bounce hit the ground he bounced high into the air again. He bounced past Mr Tickle, right to the top of the tree!

Next Mr Tickle went to the boating lake. Mr Worry was in a rowing boat in the middle of the lake.

Mr Tickle stretched out his arm and tickled Mr Worry. Mr Worry dropped his oars. They disappeared into the lake.

'Oh dear,' said Mr Worry. 'How am I going to get back without any oars?'

Mr Tickle stretched out his arm again. He pulled the boat to the edge of the lake. Soon Mr Worry was back on dry land.

On the other side of the lake Mr Wrong was feeding crumbs to the swans.

'I'm feeding the hens,' said Mr Wrong.

'Those are swans, not hens,' said Mr Tickle.

Then Mr Tickle reached out a long arm to tickle one of the ducks. The duck was cross. It pecked Mr Tickle's finger.

'It serves you right,' said Mr Wrong. 'Parrots don't like being tickled!'

Some of Mr Tickle's friends were playing hide and seek in the woods.

Mr Sneeze hid in a clump of ferns. But Mr Happy heard him sneezing and found him.

Mr Nosey hid behind a bush. But Mr

Happy saw his nose sticking out among the leaves.

Mr Skinny hid in the grass. He lay very still. Then a long arm reached out and tickled him. He leapt up and Mr Happy saw him straight away.

In another part of the park, Mr Tickle found Mr Strong and Mr Forgetful playing with a bat and ball. Mr Forgetful had forgotten what to do with the bat. Mr Strong reminded him.

'You are supposed to hit the ball with the

bat,' Mr Strong explained.

Mr Strong was about to throw the ball when something tickled him. The ball flew out of his hand and over to the greenhouse.

SMASH! went a window. Mr Tickle ran away as fast as he could!

Inside the greenhouse Mr Silly was smelling all the flowers. Then something tickled his head. Mr Silly looked round. All he could see was a tall plant with prickly leaves.

'It's a tickling plant!' cried Mr Silly.

He did not see Mr Tickle hiding behind a plant pot.

Mr Silly told everybody that he had been tickled by a tickling plant. But nobody believed him.

Later Mr Tickle found Mr Daydream sitting on a bench in the rose garden.

Mr Daydream was daydreaming again. In his dream he was sitting by the sea in a faraway country.

There was a fountain by the bench. It

made a splashing sound. Mr Daydream thought this was the sound of the waves in his dream.

Then something tickled Mr Daydream. He stopped daydreaming and looked around. Who do you think it was?

Mr Jelly was feeling very brave. He had a go on the slide in the play park! But when he got to the top he was afraid to slide down. Mr Rush was standing behind him on the ladder.

'Hurry up!' cried Mr Rush. 'I'm waiting.'

But Mr Jelly still held on tightly.

Then a long arm reached up and tickled Mr Jelly. He let go of the edge and WHOOOOSH! The next thing he knew, he was at the bottom of the slide.

Soon afterwards Mr Tickle found Mr Fussy and his friends having a picnic. They did not see Mr Tickle hiding behind a bush.

Mr Tickle tickled Mr Clumsy who was drinking some lemonade. It spilt all over

the clean white tablecloth.

Mr Fussy looked a bit upset. So Mr Tickle tickled him to cheer him up. What do you think happened to the cake Mr Fussy had in his hand?

By the end of the day Mr Tickle was very tired and thirsty. He went to the cafe for a nice cold drink.

But Mr Tickle could not keep his hands still for long. He tickled an old lady at the next table and made her spill her coffee.

He tickled the waitress and made her drop her tray!

Then it was time to go. When he got home, Mr Tickle thought about all the people he had tickled that day. There were so many that he was still trying to think of them all when he went to bed!

Questions to talk about

1. What made the gardener fall into the leaves?
2. Why did Mr Tickle have to rescue Mr Worry?
3. Who was looking for Mr Tickle's friends when they were hiding? Did he find them all?
4. Who broke the greenhouse window?
5. Do you think that any plants can tickle?
6. Who was waiting behind Mr Jelly on the slide?
7. Can you remember all the people Mr Tickle tickled?